Patricia Heitz
52 Egmont Ct.
Delmar, NY 12054
www.patriciaheitz.com

Book Layout © 2017 BookDesignTemplates.com

Daydreams Come True/Patricia Heitz -- 1st ed.
ISBN 978-0-578-19754-8

Professional Dedication

The information contained in this book is information summarized from many authors who have blessed our world by sharing what they have learned. I follow their lead by sharing what has helped me heal my life and create a Daydream Come True Life.

However, the foundation of this book originally came from two very selfless people, Gail Straub and David Gerson, who wrote a book called *Empowerment* and who are dedicated to teaching these empowerment principles through their Empowerment Institute in Rhinebeck, New York. I was privileged to be one of their students and was blessed to have them give me their book and an outline to go out and empower the world!

Personal Dedication

I dedicate this book to my family, my husband, son, and daughter, who have loved me unconditionally and supported me fully during all my life changes, through sickness, health, anger, and healing.

Preface

My amazing journey of learning started in 2002 when I heard these words: "You have a mass on your kidney". I was dumbfounded. I had no symptoms. At the time, my children were 14 and 6. I kept thinking "My children are young; this cannot happen to me!". My father-in-law had just died from this same disease, kidney cancer, only 10 months prior. It seemed like more than a coincidence to me. I felt there was something I needed to learn from this. My daily prayer during the process of treatment and post-surgery was "Help me see what I need to see and know what I need to know". Every day I prayed this prayer believing there was something more I needed to know about this disease in my body.

During this time, someone gave me the book "You Can Heal Your Life" by Louise Hay. When I read the book, and came upon this question "Why do you need this?", the answer hit me like a bolt of lightning! I suddenly knew why this disease was in my body. The answer overwhelmed me, and I broke down in tears as I realized what I had done to myself in my self-hate, and feeling of not deserving and guilt. I had held on to so much anger and negative energy that allowed this disease to grow in my body. From that moment on, I knew I had to learn more about mind, body wellness and its connection to disease.

I learned after the biopsy the cancer was completely encapsulated in the kidney and it had shut down as the tumor started to grow. This meant the cancer cells could not metastasize in my body. Now, I felt I had been given another chance; a chance to learn how to create happiness in my life instead of disease. I read every mind, body wellness book, listened to every tape, CD or audio I could find on this subject. I had many "aha" moments that were inspiring, motivating and sometimes painful.

Growing up in an alcoholic household and forming a belief system about not being good enough, or deserving of happiness, I found, was the foundation of my self-negating beliefs. I learned I had attracted many negative and sometimes abusive people, situations and events into my life, that supported my low self-esteem and that I believed I just had to suffer through. By understanding these beliefs, where they came from, how to find forgiveness for both myself and those who helped me form those beliefs, I was able to put into action a formula for living a happy, dream-come true life!

One of the habits I had created in childhood to escape a difficult home life was to daydream. I would escape into a happier place, home and situation. I had utilized this habit throughout my life prior to my kidney cancer diagnosis and it always brought me what I daydreamed. However, what sabotaged me was my belief system. I could attract what I wanted, but the heartbreak was when I wasn't able to maintain it. There was always a feeling of disbelief; always a little voice in my head that questioned if this was right for me to have. This is when it would all come crashing down and I would find myself in a difficult, painful situation once again.

When I started studying all the principles of Law of Attraction, self- love and mind body wellness, I discovered how to recognize my self-sabotaging beliefs. This is when my life truly changed. I recognized why the abusive person was in my life; why I had to declare bankruptcy after being successful, why I had to keep myself away from loving people and attracted negative people; why I had cancer in my body.

This book is the culmination of all I have learned over the last 15 years of discovering who I ready am and changing my belief system from one of "I don't deserve this" to "I deserve everything I have ever wanted and more." My hope is you too, will find your true self through this book and transform your belief about yourself into one of self-love, acceptance and great happiness. Utilizing the steps of focused daydreaming, release of negative beliefs and therefore creating the space for passionate belief in your dream, you too can start living your Daydreams Come True Life!

Introduction

What are daydreams?

"A daydream is a visionary fantasy experienced while awake, especially one of happy, pleasant thoughts, hopes or ambitions.

Eric Klinger. Psychology Today. October 1987

Daydream

A usually nonpathological reverie that occurs while a person is awake. The content is usually the imagined fulfillment of wishes that are not disguised.

Mosby's Medical Dictionary, 8th edition. © 2009, Elsevier.

What do you daydream of? When you find your mind wandering, what fantasy do you allow yourself to dream; or do you allow yourself to daydream? Daydreams are, if we allow ourselves to have them, our thoughts about what we would like to have or be in our lives. They can be just mindless thoughts, or they can be powerful tools to help you live the life you have always wanted.

What dreams do you or have you had that you wish would come true? Do you remember them? Did you tuck them away for fear they would never come true?

Do you dream of the perfect relationship, where you are loved unconditionally by that special someone with whom you would live happily ever after? Or, do you dream about the perfect job with the perfect boss and the abundant paycheck? Is it your dream home? Take a moment and close your eyes and envision that dream. What does that picture look like? What does it feel like? Whatever your dream, know you can attain it through the focused practice of daydreaming!

Many in the past have looked at daydreams as just fantasies that your mind wanders to when you are bored. However, if you pay attention to these thoughts, they will show you what your heart desires. If you practice utilizing these daydreams as focused thoughts to create what you want in your life, they can be your roadmap to reality.

The *secret* of bringing a dream to full and lasting manifestation is not only a focused attention to your dream, but also the awareness and release of any negative beliefs you may have that can create roadblocks.

You may be able to bring your dream or portions of your dream into reality just by focused attention on it, but if your beliefs about yourself are clouded by *any* negativity—if your underlying belief system is negative—it will eventually sabotage you. This workbook is about first, helping you identify, envision, feel, and plan for the emergence of your dreams, and secondly, to help you clear any negative beliefs you may not be aware of that could eventually sabotage the permanent residence of your dreams come true. This book will help you to understand what you really want, what your true beliefs are about yourself, what your true potential is, and how to create a daily practice that will make your dreams come true!

I have utilized daydreaming most of my life, unknowingly, to create more of what I wanted in my life. Daydreaming was an escape from an unhappy home situation that became not just a way to cope with all the negativity around me but, as I matured, I realized these daydreams became a strong map for where I wanted to go and they helped propel me to happier places. However, my belief system worked in contradiction to my daydreams and I would soon find myself pulled backward. Not until I learned to pay attention to the repetition of these patterns did I discover how to heal and transform my negative belief system to create a happy, prosperous, peaceful, and content life by using my daydreams and healing my belief system. This book is the manifestation of my own daydreams through many painful epiphanies and lessons learned. This book will help you, as much as you allow, to use daydreams to create your dream-come-true life!

Before we begin, I must tell you that to proceed, you MUST make these agreements with yourself

1. You MUST commit to <u>complete honesty with yourself.</u> Without truth, nothing can be changed, because the truth will be hidden, and any attempt to move forward will be thwarted by what lies beneath.

2. You MUST be ready for the truth because if you are not ready to see what you have been hiding to yourself, you won't accept what you need to do to create your amazing new life!

There may be times when this will feel uncomfortable, maybe even painful. This is normal and to be expected and <u>always temporary</u>. This is when you will experience real change! Remember:

NOTHING CHANGES UNTIL SOMETHING CHANGES!

If you want to experience real change, you will have to commit to brutal honesty! Are we in agreement? Ok, then let's proceed!

Courage doesn't always roar. Sometimes courage is the little voice at the end of the day that says I'll try again tomorrow.

– MARY ANNE RADMACHER

Attitude is Everything
(Author Unknown)

There once was a woman who woke up one morning,
looked in the mirror,
and noticed she had only three hairs on her head.
Well," she said,
"I think I'll braid my hair today."
So, she did, and she had a wonderful day.

The next day she woke up,
looked in the mirror
and saw that she had only two hairs on her head.
"H-M-M," she said,
"I think I'll part my hair down the middle today."
So, she did, and she had a grand day.

The next day she woke up,
looked in the mirror,
and noticed that she had only one hair on her head.
"Well," she said,
"Today I'm going to wear my hair in a ponytail."
So, she did, and she had a fun, fun day.

The next day she woke up,
looked in the mirror,
and noticed that there wasn't a single hair on her head.
"YEA!" she exclaimed,
"I don't have to fix my hair today!"

Attitude is everything.
Be kinder than necessary,
for everyone you meet is fighting battle.
Live simply,
Love generously,
Care deeply,
Speak kindly.......

Life is not about waiting for the storm to pass, it's about learning how to dance in the rain.

- VIVIAN GREENE

CONTENTS

CHAPTER ONE

YOUR DREAM AND HOW TO FIND IT

"Do not spoil what you have by desiring what you have not; remember that what you now have was once among the things you only hoped for."

-EPICURUS (Greek philosopher, BC 341-270)

With paper and pen in hand, let's get started.

1. Write down and describe what your dream(s) looks like, (start with one and use this manual to do the same with any other dream) What is it that you really, really want?

    (Choose vivid words; draw pictures if it helps; be descriptive and specific)

2. Now close your eyes and envision this in your world.

3. Now, *feel* the excitement. Stay there for as long as you'd like...

Note: If you need to, you may use the journal pages at the back of this book.

If you are having trouble with this exercise, it may be that you have long since buried your dreams for fear of not realizing them. If this is happening, use the following exercise to help you reveal your long-buried dreams and bring them back to life.

What do you really want to **have, see, and be in your life**? (*Go ahead; there is nothing to be afraid of!*)

Take a few minutes to really ponder this...

If I were a magic genie that said, you can have three wishes, what would they be?

1.

2.

3.

So why don't you have these things in your life now? (Be honest!)

Really look at your answer to this question and BE HONEST! Can you answer that question without blame?

Who is responsible for what happens in your life?

- Is it you?
- God
- Someone else?

The answer is, of course, *you!* (It's ok if you don't agree right now or understand, that's ok, you will soon.)

Here is how most of us live our lives:

We concentrate on all the things we DON'T like in our lives.

- We continually focus on it.
- We then get angry about it.
- We continue to give it negative energy with our thoughts, actions, and words, (complaining) and, not surprisingly, it continues to happen.

Most of us know, in detail, why our lives don't work. It is these thoughts that keep each of us in the *away from* mode.

We may be motivated to make changes when it gets too bad, but they are because we are running *away from* what we don't want. All that will eventually happen is we will find ourselves in the same situation but with different circumstances because we haven't learned how to think about what we *want*. We continue to focus on *what we don't want*. The question is, how do we change that? We can change the way we think and act by creating an authentic ***vision for our life; what we want.***

This leads us *toward* what we want, which is much more powerful and inspiring. This brings us the awareness of all the possibilities in our lives. For many, this will be a huge paradigm shift.

For many of us, the first and the biggest obstacle is in not allowing ourselves to acknowledge what we really want to have, be, and see in our lives. We do this because if we don't know or acknowledge what we want, we won't feel hurt or disappointment if these things don't come to pass in our life. However, you will never see true happiness and fulfillment in your life if you don't first, envision it, and second, work daily to create and maintain it. For some who believe they will never get what they want, it is safer for them to not dream at all.

In my experience as an Empowerment Coach, I have asked many "What do you want in your life"? Often, the answer is: "I don't know". The truth is, you do know, but it is too painful to want something and believe you cannot have it. I am here to reassure you that:

YOU CAN HAVE ANYTHING YOU WANT IF YOU BELIEVE YOU CAN HAVE IT!

That's all there is to it. It sounds much easier than it is. Most of us have had so many negative experiences and disappointments; we have come to accept this as just the way our life is. NOT TRUE! I recently spoke with someone who was very proud of herself when she said, "I've learned great coping techniques." I thought: how sad that she has accepted her life, in the unhappy place it is. If this sounds familiar, you have accepted something that doesn't have to be. What is the difference between you and someone who seemingly has it all? Do you think they are better than you or you less than them? No. You, I, and them, as human beings on this earth, are all built the same, with the same possibilities, the same spirit, and the same wants, needs, and desires. The difference is that the other person knows and *believes* in what they want and that they can have what they want. You don't. Therefore, all you have to do is change how you think, change your belief system and change your words and actions. If you are a student of the Law of Attraction, you have heard this many times before. The difference here is first, you are going to learn how to practice this daily. As you stay focused daily on this dream, you will begin to notice the changes.

Secondly, you will be releasing any deeply buried negative beliefs that, in the past, became roadblocks for you.

Now, let's begin. The following exercises will highlight the areas in which you may need to do a little adjusting.

Answer all questions as best as you can:

1. How committed am I to really creating the life I really want?

2. What is the next growth area (where adjustment is needed) in my career?

3. What is the next growth area (where adjustment is needed) regarding my finances?

4. What is the next growth area in my relationship(s)?

5. What is the next growth area in my spiritually?

Your spirituality is the soul of you; the energy from a higher place that exists within and from which you draw from the higher-self that drives you. Without a sense of spirituality in your life, you are swimming upstream, making your life experience harder. Conversely, when you recognize and access this sense of spirituality, you are able to utilize a powerful energy with you that will *propel* you forward. Your spirituality will light your path and connect you with your inner power. It will keep you inspired, encouraged, and motivated during times when your lower–self and the world around you create roadblocks. Spirituality doesn't have to come in the form of religion, although for some it may. Spirituality is simply your connection to a Higher Power, God, or the Universe, whatever feels comfortable for you. The higher energy that changes the seasons, that pushes the plant up from the dirt and creates a bloom, the energy that keeps your heart beating. Part of your lesson here is to pay attention to how this Power is helping you to manifest both the negative and the positive experiences of your life depending on your daily thoughts and actions. Without your connection to this Power, you will have a harder time and miss many clues of where to go and what to do to make your life much happier and easier.

What does all this have to do with making your dreams come true? Everything! Think of your spirituality as your engine that drives you forward.

Belief System

Whomever you believe you are, whatever you believe you deserve, is what you get! Let's say that again: *whomever you believe you are, whatever you believe you deserve, is what you get*! Simply put, if you believe you are not worthy of the things you previously stated, you won't realize them in your life no matter how many times you affirm them.

Many of you who are reading this are thinking: "I do believe in myself; I do feel worthy." Now, here's the part you won't like, but remember, you have committed to honesty. *If you really believe you deserve what you want, you would have what you want.* No matter how many times you recite affirmations, read motivational books, listen to motivational tapes, etc., if your underlying belief system is in contradiction with your thoughts and actions, your belief system wins!

Now, let's review your belief system. Let's look at what you really believe about yourself and ultimately who you believe you are. If I were to ask you to describe yourself, what would your answer(s) be?

Who are you? What are your values (i.e., good person, kind, considerate, and what are your life role(s), i.e., mother, wife, husband, father, boss, friend, neighbor)?

I

am_____

_____

_____

_____

What do you say to yourself about yourself during your day?

(Note: klutz, stupid, too busy, stressed, sensitive, fat, skinny, unlucky, always broke...)

I am

_____

_____

_____

What do you say out loud or in your head about your job, your mate, your friends, your co-workers, your boss, your career, your life?

_____

_____

_____

There is one, very important Universal law you must understand and be conscious of every single day:

WHATEVER YOU THINK ABOUT AND BELIEVE ABOUT YOURSELF YOU ARE AND/OR EVENTUALLY BECOME! This is the Law of Attraction.

If you believe and say you are a klutz, then you will act as one. If you believe and say you are poor, you will be. If you believe you are too busy to enjoy the things you like/love in your life, things will always be showing up to prevent you from enjoying those things in your life. The list goes on and on. Your belief system creates who you are, and what is created in your world. Therefore, if you want your experience in life to be different, to be more fulfilling, to be happier, you must start with what you believe about yourself, including what you *say* about yourself!

When you start believing you deserve and can have what you want, you will begin to realize and see what you desire. Admittedly, this is much easier said than done. Our childhood experiences have formed our belief systems. Most of us have negative experiences in our childhood that have created negative beliefs about ourselves as adults. We make decisions in our childlike minds about negative events, situations, and people. These decisions that have a meaning to us become our beliefs. In other words, we experience a negative event and, in our childlike minds, we attach a meaning to that event, situation, etc. to try and make sense of it. Example: My mother always would say "We just have no luck." I as a child took this to mean I must be less than and don't deserve. This was her belief that she passed on to me. Consequently, our family always struggled with money as did I until I cleared and released this belief. These belief systems have come to be very *bad habits* that then create our life experiences. However, that is what they are; bad habits that can be changed if you are committed to creating the life of your dreams!

Remember, at the beginning of this book, I said complete honesty would be a requirement for successfully realizing your dream? Facing your underlying beliefs about yourself and being honest about them can be painful. It may bring up some things you may not want to talk or think about and have buried but is essential to true transformation. Remember, whatever comes up is temporary. Once you address it and are aware of it, you can change it. I will also tell you that the truth may not always present itself immediately. You may have to continually ask yourself the important questions, many times over for many days, before your subconscious feels safe in letting the truth present itself. When the truth does present itself, it can come as a powerful epiphany, that can take your breath away, and it may not always feel good. However, we can look at this response much like a Band-Aid applied to a cut that needs air to heal. Once ripped away, the wound is exposed and allows the healing process to begin. This is the only way. The longer you wait, the longer it takes to bring your dreams into reality.

Homework:

For optimum results, it is suggested that you do these exercises in the AM and PM.

AM:

1. Each morning during this week, rewrite in your daily calendar your dream(s). Write it/them and then say it aloud to yourself. You can do the aloud part in your car as you drive, or in the shower, or wherever you feel comfortable saying it aloud. As you do this, notice your belief system. Each time you say it, does it feel stronger? Does it feel that the "but..." is starting to dissipate? If not, just keep saying it aloud, eventually, you will start to notice a feeling of belief that this is yours to have.

You can use a Daily Prayer Meditation to keep you at a higher vibrational place throughout your day to help you be more knowing and aware. I have included below one I use. However, if this doesn't feel comfortable for you, it's fine to skip this.

"Our Father who is in Heaven, Holy be your name, your kingdom come, your will be done,_____ (fill in what you want to achieve) here on earth as it is in Heaven. Help me find and recognize your light and love in my day through the people, events, and situations you bring me. As I recognize you and your love, I am easily able to find forgiveness and healing for myself and all those I have perceived to have wounded me. Lead me only to the light and love of you and help me ignite and inspire your light in all those that I meet. As I am able to ignite my own light and inspire your love in all, light projects out to the world through me and our world is flooded with only light. As the world is flooded with light, we are able to completely banish the darkness and live in only the light of love with each other. It is then that we are able to live with you in the kingdom, power, and glory, AMEN.

PM:

1. Write your dream again in the evening and say it out loud again. Notice your belief system; do you feel any doubt or fear? Are there any "but…"? If not, you are progressing wonderfully! If there are any "buts" that come up, that's ok; you will need to explore your belief system a little more and work on transformation.

   a. Write down any situations or events that felt different that caused you to be more aware of positive situations. Include events or people that showed up in support of your dream.

   b. Write down any events or situations that you felt you contributed to negatively that were in direct opposition of your dream.

CHAPTER TWO

CREATING REAL CHANGE

Our greatest glory is not in never falling, but in getting up every time we do.
-Confucius

Now that you have defined what it is you want in your life, and discovered a bit more about your reflection of yourself and your beliefs, it is time to make some declarations and a commitment to making some real changes.

I suggest that you place the answers to these questions in the form of an intention. (*It is suggested that you purchase a journal to write your intentions in so that you may visit them frequently.*)

I intend to create_____in the area of_____.

Examples:

- *I intend to create a love of work, balance, and prosperity in my work/job.*
- *I intend to create a life filled with ease, peace, loving relationships, great abundance and prosperity in all I do.*
- *I intend to create/manifest a loving relationship with my soul mate.*
- *I intend to create wealth, prosperity and abundance demonstrated in every area of my life.*

(You can use this formula with any personal issues you would like to change as well, and be more specific about any area of your life you would like to change.)

_____

_____

_____

_____

_____

_____

_____

_____

_____

Next, it is time to test what your belief system is telling you as you make these declarations. Just identifying and declaring what you want is sometimes not enough. *Remember, if your underlying belief is in opposition to what you say you want, the underlying belief will eventually win and you will have sabotaged what you want.* Have you ever asked yourself, "Why did I do that?" when you have done something that worked against yourself? This is your underlying belief system at work. You must make sure what you really believe in is in line with what you really want. So, let's explore your belief system.

Self-responsibility

When something you have planned for does not work out, what do you say to yourself? Is your response negative? "It is _____ fault. I can't believe they did that to me." When you do this, you give your power to someone else, and you feel victimized. The truth is, you are completely responsible for everything that happens to you, even if someone else did something against you! WOW! Some of you are about ready to burn this book; please don't! Hang in there and I'll explain.

When you believe that you don't deserve something or someone, a relationship, a job, or good fortune, when any of these show up, your inner belief system conflicts with what you want, and you attract that which you *really believe* and it will sabotage you. In other words, when someone else does something to you, you actually created the situation so that you end up a victim and can place the blame on someone else. Why? There can be a number of reasons, but mostly it is: *Because it is easier to blame someone else than to take responsibility for what you believe and make the change.*

The truth is we are very powerful beings. We have this Universal Power within us to attract that which we really believe we should have. So, if your inner belief system is in opposition to what you declare you want, you will attract something or someone that will eventually create a roadblock. When we take responsibility for our experiences, we empower ourselves! The journey of life is like a big classroom filled with learning experiences. Have you had the experience of having had sabotage after sabotage happen each time you try and create something better in your life? Do you find yourself time after time saying, "Why does this keep happening?" If so, then you haven't learned what you need to learn from these situations, and they will continue. Once you take responsibility for them, acknowledge what the lesson is, and learn the lesson from a situation, it will stop occurring in your life and you will no longer keep repeating the lesson!

Here is an example from my life experience. I had a difficult relationship with my mother. Somehow, it seemed that in every job, there was always one woman who was difficult to deal with, someone who would give me a hard time. I couldn't figure it out—every job, always a woman with the same personality, presenting the same difficult relationship for me.

When I started studying human potential and self-empowerment, I finally realized that the relationship between my mother and I had not been resolved. Until I could resolve it and forgive, my mother kept showing up everywhere I worked! When I finally released and forgave my mother, that difficult situation stopped occurring. The lesson is, whatever unresolved issues we harbor in our lives, they will continue to show up until we resolve them. Ask yourself this: does anything keep repeating over and over in your life? What do you need to release and forgive?

Self-esteem

Do you believe you are:

- Lovable?

- Confident in your abilities?

- Worthy of a happy and abundant life?

Most of us have a negative self-image that is a result of childhood issues not yet resolved, lessons not yet learned, and people and situations we have not yet forgiven. We can blame and continue to give our power away, or we can explore not the *why*, but the *what is next* version of our life. As long as you stay in blame for something that has happened, it will continue to stay with you.

Some of you may have an epiphany regarding your core beliefs. As a result, you will need to think about it for a while to see how it affects your everyday life. That's OK. But don't get stuck there. Take the information you need, recognize the lesson you need to learn, learn it, and move on!

Remember, when you have ANY self-negating attitudes and do nothing to change them, you will undermine yourself in those areas of your life where you feel most negative. At work, you may perform just fine, but not so fine when it comes to your relationships. Or, you may be great with relationships, but always have financial problems. Each one of us has labeled ourselves in a particular way. If you say about yourself "I am stupid" this will show up as not understanding things. If you say about yourself "I am not good with relationships" this is translated into your underlying belief of "I'm not lovable." This is most likely a message from a parent or caregiver that shows up in many ways, always relationship-oriented, at work, relationships with family members, lovers, siblings, and friends. If you say about yourself "I could never have that" this is translated into your underlying belief of "I don't deserve it." This is most likely a childhood message that manifests negativity in a variety of ways: relationships, money, job/career.

Trust in the Universe

Do you believe we are all a part of a larger Universe that is supportive and benevolent; a Higher Intelligence that cares for you, one you can turn to in times of need?

Those who trust in the Universe/ God /Higher Power, (whatever feels true for you) and embrace this spiritual connection, feel supported in life and enjoy a sense of security. Those who don't believe or embrace their spirituality believe they are alone in this life. They are continually trying to protect themselves and move through life with caution and fear. Those who trust in the Universe are willing to take risks and feel the full pulse of life. They are not gripped by fear and live their lives with inner peace. These are the people who are the happiest and the most successful in life.

Positive Attitude

Do you believe the glass is half full or half empty? Are problems opportunities from which to learn or just continuous annoyances?

Definition of a person with a positive attitude:

*Looking at the reality of a problem, the **real** truth, straight in the eye and seeing what can be constructively created from each situation.*

This takes courage and strength.

Below are some questions that will take a lot of courage to answer. If you are not ready, it's ok to come back to this. These questions will help you identify what beliefs you have that lie beneath so you can turn them around:

- Do you find the possibility of good in something negative?

- In times of stress, how do you act?

- Do you blame others, deflect responsibility, and give away your power to change things, get depressed, blame yourself, and get angry? If so, these are all part of your underlying beliefs that must change in order to live your dream life.

- Is it fear that blocks you from taking responsibility?
    o What are you afraid of?

- Is it blame that prevents you from finding your own power and a solution?

- Could you change this belief of looking at what could go wrong to one of what could go right?

- Could you focus on what you want to happen in the situation instead of what you don't want to happen in the situation?

- What would happen if it did go wrong?
  o Could you fix it?

By believing in the power of _**you**_, you can change the outcome by exploring all the possibilities instead of all the difficulties. Create a commitment to change that belief and change the outcome.

Flowing with Change

Do you get upset when something unexpected occurs? Do you become anxious when circumstances change and you can't control them? Remember, it is the nature of the Universe to change. *Growth requires change*. So many of us resist change and often long for things to stay as they are even if they don't serve us. You will never see growing things in nature, in your garden, in the world that do not change as they grow. You are physically changing every day throughout your life. All of us grow older and watch how our bodies change. Change is evolution. Change is wonderful!

"When you're green, you grow and when you're ripe, you rot."

-Ancient Zen proverb

"And the time came when the risk to remain tight in a bud was more painful than the risk it took to blossom."

-Anais Nin

We stay in the negative because what we know is more comfortable than what we don't know, even if what we know is painful. Fear of the unknown is most often more fearful than staying in pain.

Summary:

To further explore the areas of your belief system, make a list of what needs to change. To do this, ask yourself these questions:

Do I believe in myself?

- What needs to change?

- How is this apparent in my daily life?

- What can I do to believe in myself more?

How much do I believe the Universe (i.e., God, Universal Intelligence, life force, or whatever words you choose) supports me?

- How does this affect my daily life?

- What can I do to develop more trust in a supportive Universe?

Do I approach life mostly positively or mostly negatively? (Do I look at the proverbial glass half full or half empty?)

- How does this show up my daily life?

- How can I be and think more positively?

- How can I accept change and flow with change more easily?

- In what areas of my life do I find it the most difficult to flow with and accept change?

Really think about the answers to these questions. I don't have the answers for you, only you have the answers. However, if you really think about your answers and pay attention to what comes up, you will know exactly what you must do. Take time for the truth of your answers to show up. When the answers come, they may be upsetting; that's ok, but don't dwell. Most likely, the first answers that pop into your head are the correct ones. However, if answers don't come easy, it is ok. Take a few days or even a few weeks to really think. Frequently, when you get an "I don't know" answer, there is a part of you that doesn't want to know; that is your fear. Tell yourself it is OK and it is safe to know the answer. This is the only way to heal the wounds, move past them, and find the freedom to make your dreams come true.

Homework:

AM:

1. Each morning during the week of this lesson, rewrite in your daily calendar your dream(s). Write it/them and then say it aloud to yourself. You can do the aloud part in your car as you drive, or in the shower, or wherever you feel comfortable saying it aloud. As you do this, notice your belief system. Each time you say it; do you notice it is stronger than the previous lesson? Is the *believing* piece getting stronger? Does it feel that the "but…" is starting to dissipate? If not, just keep saying it out loud, eventually the *believing* becomes *knowing*, that this is yours to have.

If you choose, use your Daily Prayer Meditation to keep you at a higher vibrational place throughout your day to help you be more aware and knowing.

DAILY PRAYER MEDITATION – If you choose

PM:

1. Write your dream again in the evening and say it out loud again. Notice your belief system; do you feel any doubt or fear? Are there any "but…"? If not, you are progressing wonderfully! If there are, you may need to go back and rework the exercise to unearth underlying beliefs that are still there.

a. Write down any situations, events that felt different, that caused you to be more aware of a. positive situations, events or people that showed up in support of your dream. See if you can catch yourself thinking more positively, using more positive words and, therefore, attracting more positive people, events, and situations.

b. Write down any events, situations, that you felt *you* contributed to negatively that was in direct opposition of your dream.

CHAPTER THREE

CLEARING NEGATIVE BELIEF PATTERNS

The greatest griefs are those we cause ourselves.

-SOPHOCLES- *Oedipus Rex*
Greek tragic dramatist (496 BC - 406 BC)

When you discover what it is you must do, be aware that a sense of fear may surface. This is how you will know you are really on your healing path. This fear is typically buried deep within, covered over by many different layers. Remember, we all have deep beliefs that, if not checked, will sabotage our path forward.

To really make these changes in your life, you must recognize the negative belief patterns that have contributed to your life thus far. Have you ever found yourself asking "Why did I say that" or "Why did I do that"? To move forward, to create real transformation, you will need to start paying attention to your patterns; patterns that may not have served you. These will lead you to those underlying negative beliefs that you must heal/release.

These beliefs come from an unconscious sense of lack of love for ourselves and most fit into three categories:

- I'm not good enough. (Don't feel confident)
- I don't have what it takes. (Fear)
- I don't deserve it. (Low self- esteem)

Most of our fears and wounds revolve around these three beliefs created from decisions made in our childhood. We cannot manifest a new belief if we are secretly holding on to an opposing belief. It is very important to pay attention to opposing beliefs that we have created to protect ourselves. They will start to come up as you start to find your truth and really pursue your dreams.

The process of change is:

The Four R's

1. **Recognition of the problem** - Stop thinking about what you *don't want* and recognize it as a problem in need of a solution. ***Think about what you DO WANT.*** Remember, there are always solutions! One of them might be just acceptance for the moment. You will be amazed at how the simple act of acceptance, surrender, and release (that which resists, persists) creates an entire shift in your feeling about it. When that happens, and you truly accept this is how it is for *right now*, (not permanently) and recognize how you can live with this better, *(for now)* you will see an improvement quickly!

2. **Realization** - Understanding of what you did to create it. This is the proverbial light bulb going off in your head! When that realization hits you, it can sometimes hit hard! I've known people to become physically ill from realizing the real meaning of their self-sabotage. However, the next step is the most important...taking responsibility for it. Whew! A big one, but where your true power lies!

3. **Responsibility** - Once you understand what you have created, and why you have created it, you can now STOP! This is powerful!

   However, the most important piece of this is: *FORGIVING YOURSELF!* Once you understand how you have created your problems and difficulties, you must take full responsibility and heal yourself. Be kind to yourself. We all create situations and attract people into our lives that do not serve us. Recognize that you have not done anything that others haven't done. It is part of being human. It's OK. Just recognize it, be aware of it, and then let it go! Many people get stuck here. They wallow in what they have done. If you do this, you cannot move forward. Although this may take some practice, the more you do it, the easier it becomes.

4. **Response** - Instead of RE-action (which basically means you re-enact the negativity) you can now respond in PRO-Action manner (moving forward). Understand the concept of the word Reaction. The dictionary defines it as "bodily, mental, or emotional response to a stimulus." (We will discuss the energy of "e-motion" a little later).

You need to move past what has happened and constructively correct the problem in a positive way through:

- Vision Creation – construct a very clear picture of what you *do want.*

- Mental Clearing – clear out all and any limiting beliefs.

- Affirmation with Visualization – daily focus on the vision of what you want along with your affirmation stating this is already here. (We'll talk more about creating affirmations a little later.)

Change is always scary, but the only path to growth. Nothing in nature can grow without change and the human being is part of the natural world. The butterfly that started as a caterpillar had to change before it could fly. You too, can find that same transformation in your life if you make that commitment to yourself. I promise you, if you make the commitment to change, and become fully aware, daily, of what you do to thwart yourself on this new journey, have the courage to see it, and take a stand to *move forward anyway,* you will quickly have the life you deserve and want!

The Final Analysis

…If you are kind, people may accuse you of selfish, ulterior motives; **be kind anyway**.

If you find serenity and happiness, they may be jealous; **be happy anyway.**

The good you do today, people will often forget tomorrow; **do good anyway.**

Give the world the best you have, and it may never be enough; **give the world the best you've got anyway.**

You see, in the final analysis, it is all between you and God;

It was never between you and them anyway.

-St Mother Teresa of Calcutta

Here are a few tips for managing any negativity that may come up on your journey.

Ten Steps for the Management of Negative Emotions

1. STOP – Take several deep breaths. This will start to calm your body so you can think more logically.

2. Allow yourself time to come down from the adrenaline rush. *(Depending on the intensity of the emotion, it may take up to 20-30 minutes—you may have to politely make an excuse to leave so you can gather your calm).*

3. Think – outside the emotion. Think logically. Remember, if you are reacting, you are not thinking logically.

4. Ask yourself —

   a. What does this *really mean* to me?

   b. Is this true, my perception, or does it not mean what I think?

5. Think, why?

   a. Why did this person, event situation present this to me?

   b. Why would I need to have this?

   c. Should I be learning something?

        d.   What is the lesson?

6. Close your eyes and picture yourself above, looking down on yourself. If you were a good friend of yours, what advice would you give—BE HONEST!

7. Think why (logically) a person may do something like this (to you). Think empathy and understanding—this has nothing to do with you! This is their stuff; everyone has a story.

8. What is the best way to proceed—logically?

9. Let go of the negativity surrounding this event, person, and forgive. *(Why would you need to hold on to this? If you continue to hold on to it, you are choosing to have it rule you in a negative way. Ask yourself how does it serve you?)*

10. Think in a positive, forward manner. Thoughts are energy. Therefore, think of something that gives you joy, makes you laugh and makes you feel good. Remember the Law of Attraction; what you keep thinking about, you will attract, bring to you and perpetuate.

WHAT DO YOU WANT TO BRING TO YOUR LIFE? (Write it down)

_____

_____

_____

_____

_____

_____

_____

_____

_____

_____

Homework:

AM:

1. Each morning during this weekly lesson, rewrite in your daily calendar your dream(s). Write it/them and then say it aloud to yourself. You can do the aloud part in your car as you drive, or in the shower, or wherever you feel comfortable saying it aloud. As you do this, notice your belief system. By now your belief system should be transforming from believing into *knowing.* If there are any beliefs still left that need transformation, go back to Lessons 1 and 2 and repeat.

You can if you choose, use your Daily Prayer Meditation to keep you at a higher vibrational place throughout your day to help you be more aware and knowing.

PM:

1. Write your dream again and again say it aloud. Your *knowing* should be stronger than any negative belief. By now, your belief system should be transformed into *knowing.* If there are any that need to be transformed go back to Lessons 1 and 2 and repeat.

2. Write any negative situations that you encountered during this lesson time. What did you do differently, think of differently, perceive differently? Were you more aware? Did you act or react in a different way?

    a. What could you have done differently?

    b. How could you have transformed it with love?

    c. Did you also notice any positive people, situations, and/or events that showed up in support of your dream?

CHAPTER FOUR

HOW TO LIVE A DREAM-COME-TRUE LIFE

The Manifestation of Daydreams into Reality!

"When you cease to dream, you cease to live."

- MALCOLM S. FORBES

Now that you have explored and released (or are in the process of releasing) any negativity in your belief system, you can move forward into creating what you really want in your life!

Remember this very important Universal Rule and *practice it daily*:

OUR THOUGHTS AND BELIEFS CREATE EVERYTHING THAT HAPPENS IN OUR LIFE.

This simple Universal Law of Attraction, just like the Law of Gravity, it is part of our experience and our daily life. Knowing how to utilize and master this law is what will help you create your dream come true life. Whatever you think about expands in your life. So, if you think negative, you get negative. If you think positive, you get positive. Anytime you have an *e-motion* you are expressing: *energy in motion = e-motion.* Emotions break down into two main energy paths which are the two most powerful. They energize our world, with people, situations, events that reflect our *energy in motion. They are love and fear. These are the two main emotions in our lives.*

Love brings us:

- Joy
- Prosperity
- Abundance
- Healing.

The lack of love (fear) creates a void in our lives that starts to fill us with:

- Depression
- Sadness
- Loneliness, and most of all
- Fear - which then creates anger

(All negative energy comes from fear/ lack of love.)

The next time you have a strong emotion, ask yourself: is this positive or negative? Is this because I sense a lack of love? If so, how can I infuse this feeling with love, the eternal healing balm for any wound created from lack of love?

- Whatever we fear and give continual thought energy to (an e-motion, *energy in motion)* we attract. As a negative e-motion, we then continue to see situations, relationships deteriorate and become worse...more of the same. Your thoughts are the movie of your life. They create the reality in your world.

- Whatever we continually think about with love, our *energy in motion* (e-motion) attracts. We will start to notice more loving people, situations, and events show up in our lives.

Whatever we put into this world is what we get out of it. The saying goes: garbage in, garbage out. Everything that happens in our lives begins with our thoughts. Therefore, if you are driving to work and are thinking negative thoughts about a spouse, boss, co-worker, family, member, etc. don't be surprised when something negative happens with that person. Negative thinking attracts negative events, situations, and people.

However, on the plus side, if something negative occurred between you and any of these people in your life, you could turn that around by thinking good thoughts about these people. ***Think of three things you like about them.*** Focus on that thought, and soon you will find the negativity you had been feeling will begin to dissipate. If you find it hard to think of something positive about them, just turn your thoughts to ANYTHING that brings you joy. Think of the laugh you had with a friend, or something joyful that recently happened to you. Then, when you are feeling more joyful, go back and think about something positive about this person you are upset with. This will create a positive energy connection regarding that person. Don't be surprised when they, unexpectedly, begin to respond to you positively. Remember, positive thoughts attract positive events. This applies to every aspect of your life, not just people. It applies to events, situations, work, relationships and finances. Understanding this fundamental principle of the Universe is essential to manifesting what you want in your life, as it begins with your thoughts.

I realize it is hard to do when you are in the e-motion of it! However, if you will give yourself time for your mind and body to detach from the emotion you are feeling, by focusing on something positive, it is much easier to do. Sometimes, if you can't bring yourself to think positive about the person or event, by changing your thought to something else that brings you joy, you will be able to connect with the positive energy you need to bring about the change. Focusing on something that can bring a smile to your face will erase the negative energy and, before you know it, you will be able to think a better thought about that person or event.

The key is to become aware when something negative happens, and you begin to feel that negative emotion. Stop engaging in the negative thoughts and do something else. Do something that helps you feel positive energy. Some may find it from listening to upbeat music, or some will find it by calling a good friend who makes you laugh or watching a funny movie; anything that takes you out of that negative emotion. Physiologically, it is impossible to be logical when you are in the state of negative emotion. This comes from our built in "flight or fight" response. When we are stimulated by fear (based on our core belief system), our body produces a cocktail of chemicals, among them, adrenaline, the very substance that works to defend us. In times of stress, we are programmed to either "fight" the threat, or "flee" from the threat. That chemical response takes blood away from our vital organs, re-focuses our sight, makes our heart beat faster and basically takes over our physical state. After the perceived threat is over, it takes at least 20 minutes to come out of this state and back into our normal state. Therefore, it is virtually impossible for us to think clearly and logically when we are in a negative emotional state. Once negative emotions subside and we are once again able to logically evaluate a situation, we can look at it without the negative emotion and choose a more positive solution.

The Process of Manifestation

The manifestation process begins with our thoughts, gains power when it appears in written form, is verbalized, and finally, is put into action. By thinking it, writing it and speaking it, we begin to create the opportunities we desire. Everything in this world is comprised of energy. Negative events, thoughts, people and situations have a lower frequency and, therefore, attract a lower frequency of negative energy. If your thoughts are positive, a higher vibrational frequency, we attract a higher frequency of positive energy.

Your thoughts emit energy as does your voice. When you create a thought, you evoke emotion, or an e-motion—energy in motion. This energy (e-motion) is either negative or positive, and it attracts like responses. Your voice gives this frequency additional energy. Therefore, speaking your positive thoughts give it more power. When you change your way of thinking (e-motions) to positive and reinforce your thoughts by verbalizing them, you will start to notice positive events beginning to develop! As you have now released any negative beliefs from your work in previous chapters, you will start to see these positive events become more lasting. Do not worry if, at first, you don't fully believe this concept. (I didn't.) Nonetheless, keep trying, and you will begin to experience the positive effects of your positive thoughts. You will then become a believer! It happens when your mind, soul, and heart come together in belief that the real power begins. When these opportunities present themselves, you then need to take the next step and act.

Many people work hard to change their thinking, clear out their negative beliefs and follow the process right up to the action part. When the opportunities begin to materialize, they are so afraid of the power of what they have created; they get scared and fail to act. Remember, you are a child of the Universe and you deserve everything you want to have in your life! The Universe supports you in everything you do, both negative and positive. You already know how the Universe supports negative beliefs by the negative things that have happened in your life, so you know this works. Now begin to apply this process to what you really want and now know you deserve. Let's look at a few examples so you can understand the concept.

Let's say you are in a conversation about work and you always say, "I can never find a job that pays me enough." One day, you decide you've had enough and go job hunting. Quickly, you become discouraged when you cannot find a job that is equivalent or better to the one you already have. You must think "What am I thinking or believing to make this happen"? That's right, you've unconsciously put that belief out into the world, and, in turn, the Universe follows your command, and so you are unable to find a better job.

Let's look at relationships. If every time you meet a new potential mate you think, maybe this is the one, but say, "I'm not very good at relationships," you won't be! Or shortly after the honeymoon period comes to an end, you find yourself becoming, once again, the victim, or you find yourself upset about the little things he/she does (The list can go on.). When the relationship falls apart, you find yourself saying again "I told you I'm not good at relationships!" It all becomes a self-fulfilling prophecy!

Now, let's change it around. The next time you catch yourself saying negative things, turn it around and say, "I have a job that gives me great joy, and pays me more than enough money for all my material wants and needs." Start saying this every day as if this job already exists. (It's ok if you are not quite sure in the belief area yet; just keep doing it, soon you will!) When you keep saying this, two things happen. First, any negativity buried within your belief system will come into your thought process. Recognize it, and release it. It will probably come in the form of "but...." Release any buts; they don't serve you. Second, with the repetition of your affirmation, your belief system starts to accept it. The Law of Attraction works on energy. Therefore, to give this energy more intensity, when you start to believe you can really have this, start to really *feel it. Feel* the excitement of it as it is here! The Universe takes direction from this feeling and your thoughts, beliefs, and statements, whether they are in the present or future, and you start to see things show up. When they show up, you need to now act. Go looking for a new job while saying this every day, and watch for the opportunities that start to show up! Here is where your belief system needs to kick in. If you haven't already released a negative belief, you can get stuck here as the part of you that doesn't believe you deserve this does something to sabotage the opportunity.

Make sure you regularly check your belief system to make sure you are confident in receiving that which you are putting out there to the Universe!

Let's take a moment to do a check:

When you think of what you want, what feeling do you get? Is it excitement? Great! Then you are ready to receive what you desire. Is it fear? Is there a little voice that says "No, I don't think so," or something similar? If so, you have some work to do in the belief department. Go back to the previous information on belief about the why of you thinking you shouldn't have this. Do the same with your relationships, finances, anything you want to be better in your life. Start by declaring to the Universe, *aloud*, what you want, as if you already have it, and then feel how great this feels when it comes. Now watch the opportunities show up! Just remember to keep repeating your belief checks to make sure you have cleared any resistance. Remember, you cannot manifest what you want *until and unless you define what that is*! We are all experts in defining what we DO NOT WANT, but when it comes to defining what you really DO WANT, we get lost. If this is happening to you, understand that this is your fear that protects you from being hurt. You don't have to put a specific label on what you want, just identify the components of what you want. The Universe will take care of the specifics and label it for you as you go. It will become clear to you.

Here are some questions to help you:

- What is my passion?

- What are my priorities?

- What gives me meaning?

- What is my life's purpose?

The process is: **V - A – A**

Vision – Create a vision for whatever you want in your life. Create a picture in your head that is full of details. Close your eyes and fully picture what you want, feel the feeling, smell the smells, hear the sounds; fully experience your dream. (Doesn't have to have a name yet; what are the components of the picture?)

(Be aware of any negative thinking that starts to arise leftover from years of habitual negative thinking. Release it and let it go. It does not serve you anymore!)

Affirmation - Now write down your vision in the form of an affirmation, something that you are so very thankful for. Make sure it is in the present tense.

(See it, say it, feel it…The more intense the feeling, the more energy is being attracted!)

I am_____ (write down the actions you are performing in your future vision.) Here is one I used:

> *I am grateful for the best-selling success of my Daydreams book and for all the lives it inspires as well as the all the prosperity it generates for me and my family.*

I then would envision the book, *(see it)* its cover, and see it in a book store, or someone reading it.

I felt *(feel it)* the happiness and joy in watching someone be inspired by its content.

Write down everything you experience in your vision as an event that has already happened. Always start your affirmation with "I am grateful for_____." Say this EVERY DAY!!! Even if you don't believe it, and it is not here yet, say it. Yes, it is a challenge of faith! Just say it every day, even if it doesn't feel true. When you start saying it every day, you will start believing it, and then you will start KNOWING it. This is when events, people, and situations will simply show up!

Action – Now pay attention to the events, people, situations, and the opportunities that present themselves to you and act on them! This is how you begin to KNOW it!

You are now motivated by the forward power of your *dreams* rather than the fear of your *wounds*. This is a much more powerful inspirational force!

Also, when you add gratitude for your future statement, you reinforce the joy of having it! When you have whatever it is you want, you will feel great gratitude, won't you? You need to express that gratitude as you say and envision you receiving this. When you express gratitude for it, the joy you *feel* in receiving this energizes your vision and affirmation and makes them so much more powerful!

Practice this every day and watch how your life begins to change! Take 15 minutes in the morning to envision your dream and declare your gratitude affirmation that it has already happened. Start your day every morning, before you even get out of bed, with declaring exactly how your day will go, and be grateful. "I am grateful for the ease, joy, and prosperity of this day." (Or whatever else specifically, you want to see manifest in your day) Say it over and over, and when you say it, feel the joy and happiness of experiencing a wonderful day! Pay attention to opportunities that show up to bring you there. *This is very important.*

Have you heard the joke about the man whose house was being flooded? When the nearby river started to crest, he started praying, "God, save me!" The local police came by and said, "Come with us, the river is going to flood your home!" He said, "No, I'll wait for God to save me," and he continued to pray. Then the water climbed to the first-floor window and a neighbor came by in a row boat and said, "Come with me, I'll save you." He said, "No, I'm waiting for God to save me." He continued to pray. As the water climbed higher, he had to climb onto the roof. It was then that a helicopter came by and dropped a rope down to him and yelled: "Come with us, we'll save you." Again, he said, "No, I'm waiting for God to save me." He continued to pray. Shortly after that, the water overtook him and he drowned. When he reached heaven he said to God, "Why didn't you save me?" God said, "I sent a policeman, a neighbor in a rowboat, and a helicopter, why didn't you go with them?"

Pay attention to what shows up when you use this daily practice and express your gratitude *again* when what you want shows up! Whenever you express your gratitude, you invite more of the same to come to you! Remember, sometimes what shows up is NOT EXACTLY WHAT YOU EXPECT.

The Universe likes to surprise us! However, you will find that what shows up serves you even better than what you had thought about. Recognize what shows up no matter how different it may be.

Homework:

AM:

1. Each morning during this weekly lesson, say aloud your Daily Affirmation to manifest your dream. You can do the out loud part in your car as you drive, or in the shower, or wherever you feel comfortable saying it aloud. As you do this, notice your belief system. By now your belief system should be transformed into *knowing.* If there are still any beliefs that need transforming, go back to Lessons 1 and 2 and repeat.

Use can choose to use your Daily Prayer Meditation to keep you at a higher vibrational place throughout your day to help you be more *knowing.*

PM:

1. Write in your journal how your day seemed different, now that you have a Daily Affirmation. Do you have a better sense of *knowing* that what you want is here and only awaiting the right moment? How is your day different? Did anything that has been a pattern in your life change? How? Did anything that was negative change; or did your perception of what you considered a negative event, person, or situation change? How did it change? Why did it change?

2. Write any negative situations that you encountered during this lesson time. What did you do differently, think of differently, perceive differently? Were you more aware? Did you act or react in a different way?

    a. What could you have done differently?

    b. Did you also notice any positive people, situations, and/or events that showed up in support of your dream?

CHAPTER FIVE

CREATION OF YOUR DREAM COME TRUE

"Dream your dreams with open eyes and make them come true."

-T.E. LAWRENCE

When you begin to see the opportunities, events, and people show up in your life, creating a manifestation of your dreams and affirmations, you will be motivated and inspired to continue your daily practice. This daily practice will continue to produce results. However, BE AWARE, it will take some time for your underlying belief system to be in sync with your new view of the world. You may, occasionally, find self-sabotage still at work as you may still be in the process of releasing *all* your negative beliefs. This is normal. Keep going, as it keeps getting better!

You have accumulated wounds along the way of your life, which have molded your belief system. In childhood, when you experienced something negative, not understanding, you attached a meaning to it to try to make sense of it. With the immaturity of a child, you attached meaning. It meant something very different than it would if you looked at it through the eyes of an adult. As an adult, you can now see it in a completely different view; one that is logical. Additionally, we have built up protection and a wall around that event (wound) and have buried it deep so it can't hurt us anymore. Many times, we can't even remember the event because to remember it would inflict pain and we have come to avoid pain at all costs. So now, any event, situation, or person who shows up in our lives that *reminds* us of the meaning we have attached to that initial event, produces the same pain, anger, and fear. Here are a few examples:

I grew up in a dysfunctional, alcoholic family. My grandmother was the only one who I felt gave me unconditional love. When my grandmother died, I was nine years old. I discovered when I was working this process later in life that I was so upset that my grandmother left me, I made a decision that I would never love anyone ever again. Therefore, any and every relationship of my life was, for me, one of distrust. I never allowed myself to truly and unconditionally love someone or let them love me. As a result, I had very difficult relationships with men, women, friends, and co-workers. I felt everyone always let me down because that was the meaning I attached to loving or caring for someone and have them leave. I was always angry at everyone for what I thought was their inability to show me love; yet, all the while I wasn't allowing them in. Therefore, I would always attract people into my life that weren't strong enough in their own lives to give me what I needed and, of course, would let me down only reinforcing my belief. It wasn't until I was diagnosed with kidney cancer at age 47 that I started to look at what I had created in my life. The epiphany was startling!

This anger (created from my perception of lack of love) in my mind was literally killing me! When I realized what I had created, I knew that if I wanted to live, I needed to make some important changes.

These changes, however, did not come overnight. I read every mind and body wellness book and listened to every CD on mind and body wellness I could find. I was able to bring about my own self-healing based on what I studied and learned about these principles. Right away, as I started working on this, I experienced major epiphanies! My life, within weeks, became more meaningful. However, it took me years to really be better at and change how I was doing the world. Having said that, I will tell you it may not take you that long. You may not have buried your pain as deeply as I did mine. It took me awhile to strip away layer by layer all the protection I had piled up on top of my wound. It took perseverance to know I could have a better life. Today, I am cancer free, enjoy an amazing relationship with my husband and children and find great joy in my daily life.

I know going forward, I *know* I will stay cancer free and joyful because I have healed the deep wound that created the negativity in my body, which fed the disease and my unhappiness and distrust of love.

Each person's journey is different. Yours may be easier or more difficult. It is all up to you. If you make a commitment to live a happier life, you will find it! However, be careful, from time to time, you will be tempted to revert to your old way of thinking and behaving because it is what you know and is, therefore, so comfortable and easy to return to. It is especially hard when you feel tired or stressed to revert to what you already know how to do, even if it doesn't serve you in a positive way.

It is hard to change how you think on a permanent basis. It is like going back to school to UNLEARN what you have already learned. This time, you are teaching yourself how to do the world all over again, in a different and much better way. You must learn how to release and surrender all your negative thinking and habits. This takes commitment and patience, but it is so very worth it! I now live a life that is beyond what I dreamed for myself. Back then, I couldn't even dream of all the wonderful things I have in my life now. I would probably be dead by now had I not changed my thinking to change my life!

Also know that even with the great strides and healing I have accomplished in my life, this "unlearning" is an ongoing process. I continually find other smaller wounds along the way that were attached to the big one, which I continue to heal and learn lessons from. This is a lifelong process but, as you go, the lessons get easier and easier!

Epiphany

As you daily practice your **Vision, Affirmation**, and then look for events to **Act** on, stay committed to the process. Sometimes, it takes a while before you start to see things begin to change; that's ok, just stay with it. As you progress on your journey of change and healing and start asking yourself, "Why do I need this in my life?" stay committed to the truth. Part of you, the part that wants to protect you, will prevent you from seeing the truth. Many people, as they approach real change, begin to waiver and little by little let go of their daily practice. If you find yourself in any place of fear as you go, stay on course and declare, "It is safe for me to know the answer." You must allow your subconscious to allow you the truthful answer. Remember, your subconscious is your ego, there to protect you, so keep telling yourself it is ok to know the answers. When you are ready to know, one day someone will say something, or you will be reading something, or you will be watching something on TV, or showering, etc. and your Aha moment will just happen! When you stop concentrating on the answer it will just be an amazing epiphany! The answer will just show up! You may experience pain, sadness, any of a myriad of emotions as you recognize the event that was instrumental in crafting your belief. Be kind to yourself. Depending on how deep the pain, you may experience a few days of sadness, anger, fear...this is ok. You need to let these emotions out and grieve for a process that has been a component of your entire life and that doesn't serve you anymore. You have buried them for far too long! Allow yourself time to let it go.

Now, look at the situation from a logical adult mind. If you were to have that experience as an adult, what meaning would you attach to it? You will see the illogic in your child meaning and understand it now that you are an adult. Now simply release it! Let it go! It does not serve you! You may have to do some work in forgiveness; most of us do. Many people get stuck here, as they are unwilling or unable to forgive. You may feel, as I did at first, if I forgive it is just like saying it was alright for that person to treat me as they did. However, if you put yourself in the position of that person with their own pain they were experiencing at the time, can you understand why they did what they did? Even though it was wrong of them and you don't condone what they did, can you understand why they did it? It never has anything to do with you; it is always about their pain. When you get to the place of understanding, you will be ready to let it go. Holding on to it only keeps you tied to it, victimizing you forever.

Here is an exercise to help you release.

- Close your eyes and take several deep breaths.

- Picture the pain of that event, and place it in a balloon.

- Now, release the balloon and watch it disappear out of sight.

- It is gone.

- It doesn't exist anymore.

- Let it go!

- Thank it for helping you be stronger, as you watch it disappear.

Look at your life, and ask yourself what reoccurring situations, events, or people keep showing up? Now, ask yourself if this is similar to a negative thought you have about a person, situation, or event. You may not have an answer right away. Remember, the more painful it is, the harder it is for the answer to come, but the only way to release it is to let yourself acknowledge the truth. When you do, and if it feels painful, that's ok, it's part of the healing process. Feel the pain and then release it and forgive. It is the only way to freedom!

Do this with all negative people, situations, and events that continue to show up and, one by one, they will start to be transformed! The good news is that once you do this, each time you do it for another person, situation, or event, it gets easier and easier!

Homework:

AM:

1. Each morning during this weekly lesson, say aloud your Daily Affirmation to manifest your dream. You can do the out loud part in your car as you drive, or in the shower, or wherever you feel comfortable saying it out loud. As you do this, notice your belief system. By now your belief system should be transformed into *knowing.* If there are any beliefs that need transformation, go back to Lessons 1 and 2 and repeat.

You can use your Daily Prayer Meditation for this week to keep you at a higher vibrational place throughout your day to help you be more *knowing*.

PM:

1. Write in your journal how your day seemed different, now that you have a Daily Affirmation that you believe and know.

    How is your day different? Did anything that has been a pattern in your life change? How? Did anything that was negative change; or did your perception of what you considered a negative event, person, or situation change? How did it change? Why did it change?

2. Write any negative situations that you encountered during this lesson time. What did you do differently, think of differently, perceive differently? Were you more aware? Did you act or react in a different way?

   a. What could you have done differently?

3. Take at least 30 minutes to revisit every person, situation, and event that you experienced today, especially those that were negative. Ask yourself "What did **I** do in that situation that fostered a judgmental thought or word?" Remember, even thinking of the person, situation or event in negative terms is still a judgment and sends a negative vibration out to the world that acts as a boomerang and comes back to you. It doesn't count what the other person did; only what you contributed to it. Now go back in that situation and reconstruct it again, but this time construct it with "How could I have handled this better?" Pretend that you know that this person had just received very sad or in some way, bad news, or that they have a gaping emotional wound they are trying to protect. Can you be more understanding? Remember, when someone acts in a negative emotion, they are still wounded from something. Pretend you know what that is and send them love instead of judgment.

CHAPTER SIX

MAINTAINING THE DREAM

When written in Chinese, the word "crisis" is composed of two characters—one represents danger and the other represents opportunity.

~JOHN F. KENNEDY, *Address, 12 April 1959*

Remember, that any change is not only difficult but even harder to stay with and to maintain. The old self will return for visits to tell you why this cannot be and that it is futile to keep up this daily practice or to maintain it. You may find yourself slowly, without realizing it, slipping backwards into your old belief system.

In order to make changes *permanently*, you must become aware *(mindful)* of when you find yourself slipping backward and dropping your daily practice of Vision, Affirmation and Action. You will be tempted to go backwards when in the company of family members, friends, and coworkers who have supported your OLD belief system. Your closest loved ones may even say things like, "You've changed," as if it is bad.

This is because they are not able to get the same reactions out of you that support *their* negative belief system. You need to recognize what is happening and stay on course. Be true to your dream, no matter what! The people who are bothered by your change will either adjust or leave your environment. It doesn't mean you must get a divorce, or that you must find all new friends and relatives. It simply means THEY will have to adjust to the change in you; not the other way around! You deserve this dream come true; it is your right to have it, and no one's right to say you can't. They just don't understand how it all works; be patient with them! Above all DON'T TRY AND **MAKE** THEM CHANGE! *If they ask* (and only if they ask) it is ok for you to show them what you have learned, that's wonderful. However, if they don't ask for the information, remember, thrusting your new way of doing the world on them will only make things worse and push them in the opposite direction. They must be ready to learn and want to change. However, if you allow them to infuse their negative beliefs into your fragile new world, you will start sabotaging your dream. Remember, when we hold on to painful memories, relationships, and situations because they are simply more comfortable, we cannot move forward. We stay stuck where we are. When things are more comfortable, even thoughts filled with pain, we hold on to them because we feel safe in what we know.

 Understand and recognize why you do this *(not judge)* and why others do this *(not judge),* and then let it go; it no longer serves you.

Write down what habitual people, situations, and/or events keep repeating themselves over and over in your life. Is it the choice of a mate that at first seems loving but then reveals themself as controlling and victimizing you? Is it a job or career choice you keep choosing over and over that does not serve you? Is it constant financial problems?

Whatever it is, think about what your most problematic issue is. Choose the set of questions that are appropriate for you, or maybe all are appropriate to you. Below are some questions to ponder and answer for yourself. This will require you to really think and to feel safe in the answer. If you really want to know, which is the only way to true freedom, the answer will come. However, if there is a part of you that still feels fear, the answer will elude you. Practice release.

Write a new statement that re-defines what it means without your e-motional attachment.

If you are having trouble releasing the negative, repeat the exercise from Chapter Five:

- Close your eyes and take several deep breaths.
- Picture the pain of that event and place it in a balloon.
- Now, release the balloon and watch it disappear out of sight.
- It is gone.
- It doesn't exist anymore.
- Let it go!
- Thank it for the valuable lesson it has brought to you.

If you still find some difficulty in this exercise, remember the answers are ALWAYS inside you; you KNOW the answers. However, to know the answers usually means, depending on how deep the wound is for you, to experience the original pain of the event or situation. Some of you will start this exercise and a part of you, the part that wants to protect you, will say "I don't know the answer; I don't want to know the answer". That is your ego; the protective part of you answering, not your true self who wants to learn and heal.

Here is where your commitment to find your truth and heal clashes with your ego. Here is where you will need to be committed and courageous. It is the only way to move beyond the pain and to heal. Therefore, before you begin your self-questioning, close your eyes, take one or several deep cleansing breath(s) and tell yourself, *"I AM safe, I AM loved, I AM strong."* "I want to see what I need to see and know what I need to know to heal myself". Does it feel safe to know your answers?

Ask yourself that. If it feels ok, you can start, but if there is any fear left, you will need to repeat this over and over until it feels safe. This may take a few minutes, a few hours, or a few days. That's ok, as long as you keep repeating this until you feel safe.

When you begin to get the answers to these questions, as soon as you process the answers that come up for you, write down the lesson and then a new clarified statement underneath it to transform it. You may need to take some time to do the release exercise above when the meanings of your wounds start to present themselves. That's ok, keep going! Release the memory of the pain and come back and continue this exercise.

Here is an example:

You realized by staying a victim of any person, situation or event, you get attention and it is the attention that feels good. You also realize that the underlying meaning is that you don't feel you deserve good, love, money, etc. When you reach what it means to you, your new clarified statement could be, "I AM a loved child of the Universe, born to receive love and its demonstration in my life as_____ (financial freedom, people who love me, a person who loves me, loving relationships, or whatever the issue is you need to transform).

Use this formula with:

Negative Relationship Pattern:

What does it *mean* to me to feel victimized by someone else's behavior?

Do I get sympathy, which brings me needed comfort and attention?

Do I get to reinforce my "I am not enough, or I don't deserve" belief?

What does this really *mean* to me?

Why?

What is the lesson?

What negative perception/meaning do I need to release?

Write a new, clarified statement that demonstrates what it could or could not mean without your e-motional attachment:

Negative Career/Job Pattern:

What does it *mean* to me to be constantly in jobs/positions where I either feel victimized by the job itself in doing tasks in which I feel less than or that have people in them that create a victimization feeling?

Do I get to complain to others, thereby soliciting sympathy, comfort, and attention, or does it allow me to feel part of the "tribe" of others who constantly complain about their lives where I feel I belong?

Do I get to reinforce my "I am not enough, or I don't deserve" belief?

Do you remember the first time you ever felt victimized? What was that childhood misconception that created this belief?

What does this really *mean* to me?

What is the lesson?

What negative perception/meaning do I need to release?

Write a new, clarified statement that demonstrates what it could or could not mean without your e-motional attachment:

Negative Financial Situation:

What does it mean to me to constantly feel poor? What does it mean to me that I seem to never have enough money for all the things I need and want?

Do I get to reinforce my belief that I never have enough for me because either I don't deserve or I'm not good enough? Is this about my value? (Money is value)

Am I listening to someone else's words about money that has been passed on to me as a child?

Do you remember your first feeling about money? What was it?

What was that childhood misconception that created this belief?

What does this really *mean* to me?

Why?

What is the lesson?

What negative perception/meaning do I need to release?

Write a new, clarified statement that demonstrates what it could or could not mean without your e-motional attachment:

Use this formula for any and every negative issue that seems to rule your life.

When you are finished, do you find a pattern of belief?

What is it?

When you can see the pattern, you can then see the lesson, and when you learn the lesson, you will have graduated from that issue. Once you see it, own it, and learn from it, and then you can release it. Once you release it, as you start finding yourself gravitating towards the same pattern, you will start catching yourself before you walk down the same road again. It doesn't mean you may not see any trace of the issue present itself to you again, but when/if it does, you will now be able to rise above it very quickly without e-motion. When you are able to do this, you will have truly *mastered* the lesson. This is when you will not likely experience it again.

Homework:

AM:

1. Each morning during the period of this lesson, say aloud your Daily Affirmation to manifest your dream. You can do the out loud part in your car as you drive, or in the shower, or wherever you feel comfortable saying it out loud. As you do this, notice your belief system. By now your belief system should be transformed into *knowing.* If there are any that need to reinforce this part of your homework is to go back to Lessons 1 and 2 and repeat.

You can use your Daily Prayer Meditation for this week to keep you at a higher vibrational place throughout your day to help you be more *knowing*.

PM:

1. Write in your journal how your day seemed different, now that you have a Daily Affirmation that you believe and *know*. How is your day different? Do you notice more positive events showing up to support your Affirmation? What are they?

2. Write any negative situations that you encountered during this lesson time. By using your BE-Attitude of learning from every event, did you find any lessons? What were they? What did you do differently, think of differently, perceive differently? Were you more aware? Did you act or react in a different way?

    a. What could you have done differently?

3. Take at least 30 minutes to revisit every person, situation, and event that you experienced today, especially those that were negative. Ask yourself, "What did **I** do in that situation that contributed to the negativity?" "How did my perceptions affect this situation?" "Do I have perceptions that are incorrect?" What do I need to change and learn?" Remember, even saying or thinking negative things about yourself adds more negative fuel. Things like "I am so stupid", or "I will never understand how to do this", or "I am a bad _____" (anything) just reinforces any negative self- perception and keeps you in that place. Start transforming such self-statements into: "I am learning to_____" (whatever you did that you used to label stupid), or "I am learning to understand_____and it feels good!" or "I am getting good at_____" (whatever you used to label yourself bad). Turning this around sends a positive vibration out to the world that acts as a catalyst to transform that behavior.

Daily Practice

You will need to work daily to bring about your Dream come true. Every day, if only for 10 minutes (you will find yourself wanting to stay longer as you go!) close your eyes and envision your dream. Feel how good it is, *feel* that joyful feeling of being there. Now recite your affirmation declaring this dream as a reality in your life—I AM (thankful for…, grateful for… earning my living as… living in a home that…having a loving relationship…complete financial freedom, etc. whatever states your dream in the present moment)

_____

_____

_____

Do this EVERYDAY. Keep going even if it doesn't feel true. The more you keep reciting it and feel the feeling of it being true (your vision), the more you are attracting the event, situation, or person. If it seems to take a while, that is ok. This just means there is still a part of you that doesn't really believe you deserve this and you need to be aware of what belief is preventing you from realizing this dream. Ask yourself what that belief is and tell yourself it is safe to know the answer. Keep believing; it will happen.

Finally, I have created a *Daily Daydream Development List* to help you manifest your dream. Remember to take 10 minutes minimum each day (best at the beginning of your day) to accomplish these tasks. If you make that commitment to work this list, you will find yourself living your daydream come true.

9 Steps to Manifesting Your Daydreams Come True:

1. Envision your dream.

2. Feel your dream (close your eyes and really feel how good this feels to be there)

3. Make your spiritual connection—meditate, pray, or just simply close your eyes with the feeling above and thank the Universe for the presence of this dream in your life. Stay here with that feeling and in great appreciation for as long as you can.

4. Set your Intention - Affirm/Declare —when you are ready to get going, state your affirmation as if this dream already exists.

5. Watch out for any negative feelings that arise as you continue in this process. If this happens, take a step back and ask yourself why you need to sabotage this? What do you get out of this if you stay stuck in your life without your dream come true? Keep doing this every day until you feel safe to know the answer. When you do, keep doing the above steps and the steps below every day anyway and you will release this.

6. Pay attention to opportunities in your day that start to be presented to you. Recognize them, act and always be grateful for what shows up.

7. When negative things show up (and sometimes they will), find something joyful to focus on. Stay in a positive state of mind to keep you at that higher vibrational energy, so you can move forward with your dream.

8. When you start seeing good things come to you and are living your dream, be grateful every day to keep your dream and maintain it.

9. Share it – Pass this process on! What would our world be like if EVERYONE lived their dream-come-true lives!

Conclusion

I hope this book has helped you find new beliefs of your brilliance and inner light that will allow you to have anything in your life, achieve anything you want, and make your *Daydreams Come True*.

KEEP WORKING THIS SYSTEM to keep you on track to living your dreams. In the beginning, staying on course will be your greatest challenge. Pull this book out often and keep yourself on this higher path as this is where your true happiness and dream come true is found!

Autobiography in Five Chapters - Portia Nelson

I
I walk down the street.
There is a deep hole in the sidewalk
I fall in.
I am lost...
I am hopeless.
It isn't my fault.
It takes forever to find a way out.

II
I walk down the same street.
There is a deep hole in the sidewalk.
I pretend I don't see it.
I fall in again.
I can't believe I'm in the same place.
But it isn't my fault.
It still takes a long time to get out.

III
I walk down the same street.
There is a deep hole in the sidewalk.
I see it is there.
I still fall in...it's a habit
My eyes are open; I know where I am;
It is my fault.
I get out immediately.

IV
I walk down the same street.
There is a deep hole in the sidewalk.
I walk around it.

V
I walk down another street.

I am closing with a list of BE-ATTITUDES that will help you right yourself whenever events occur that threaten to pull you back. I hope they assist you in realizing and living your dream!

Today is a result of what you believed and did yesterday, tomorrow is a result of what you believe and do today; therefore, today is **THE DAY** to make your dreams come true!

Go confidently in the direction of your dreams; live the life you have imagined

 - THOREAU

THE BE-ATTITUDES

BE *So, concerned about the improvement of yourself that you have no time to judge others…only time to be better*

BE *A student of your world and look at everything (especially the bad stuff) by what you can learn from it to improve yourself*

BE *Generous—Instead of how can I keep it, protect it, and have it make me more superior*

BE *Your own best friend—The most logical and understanding friend to yourself you could ever imagine*

BE *Spiritual*

BE *Able to let go—Forgiving of yourself and everyone*

BE *Grateful*

BE *Peaceful*

BE *Connected to your Higher Power*

BE *A healer*

BE *Fearless with love*

BE *Love*

Journal Pages

ABOUT THE AUTHOR

Patricia Heitz

Patricia is a Certified Empowerment Trainer. Her certification is from the prestigious Empowerment Institute in Rhinebeck, New York. She is a professional educator/trainer and has authored for a major publishing company in the spa industry. She owns her own consulting company and consults as a Spa Business and Training consultant. She is a licensed vocational instructor in adult education and has been teaching empowerment principles and helping empower people since 2003. Her passion for education and self-improvement is contagious, and you will feel inspired and empowered to create your own *dream-come-true* life!